crafty colouring

colouring book volume one

by claire dadswell

anything is possible...

**This edition published in 2016
by Adam Dadswell Ltd.**

All rights reserved. No part of this publication may be reproduced in any form or by any means, electronic or mechanical, including photocopying, recording or by any information storage and retrieval system, without prior written permission of the publisher.

© 2016 Adam Dadswell Ltd.

Artist: Claire Dadswell
Contents layout: imadethiscrafts.co.uk
cover design: imadethiscrafts

Printed in the United Kingdom

this book belongs to

_____

Just for fun...see if you can find the hidden objects?

Some designs have been left blank for
you to be creative, enjoy.

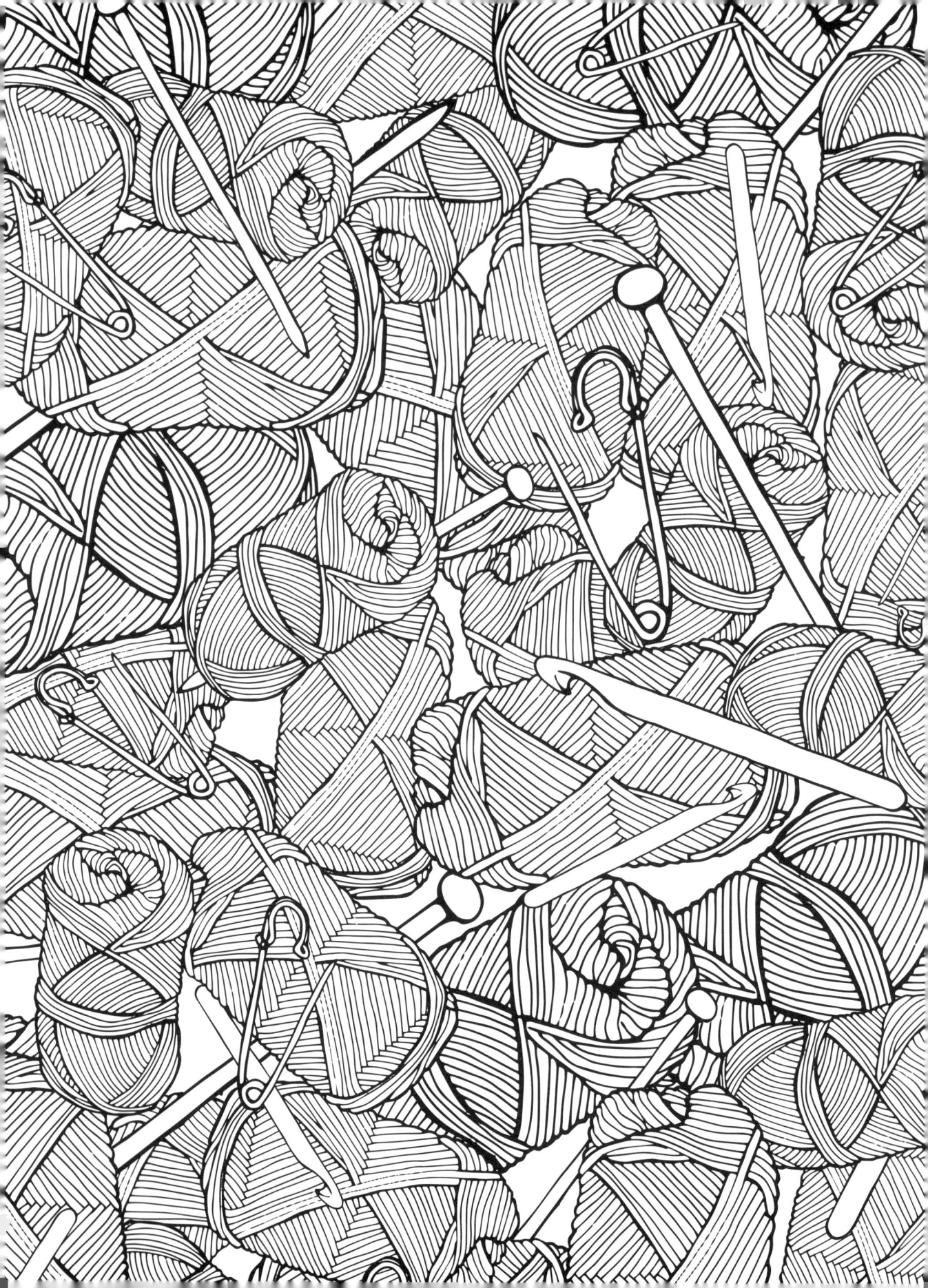

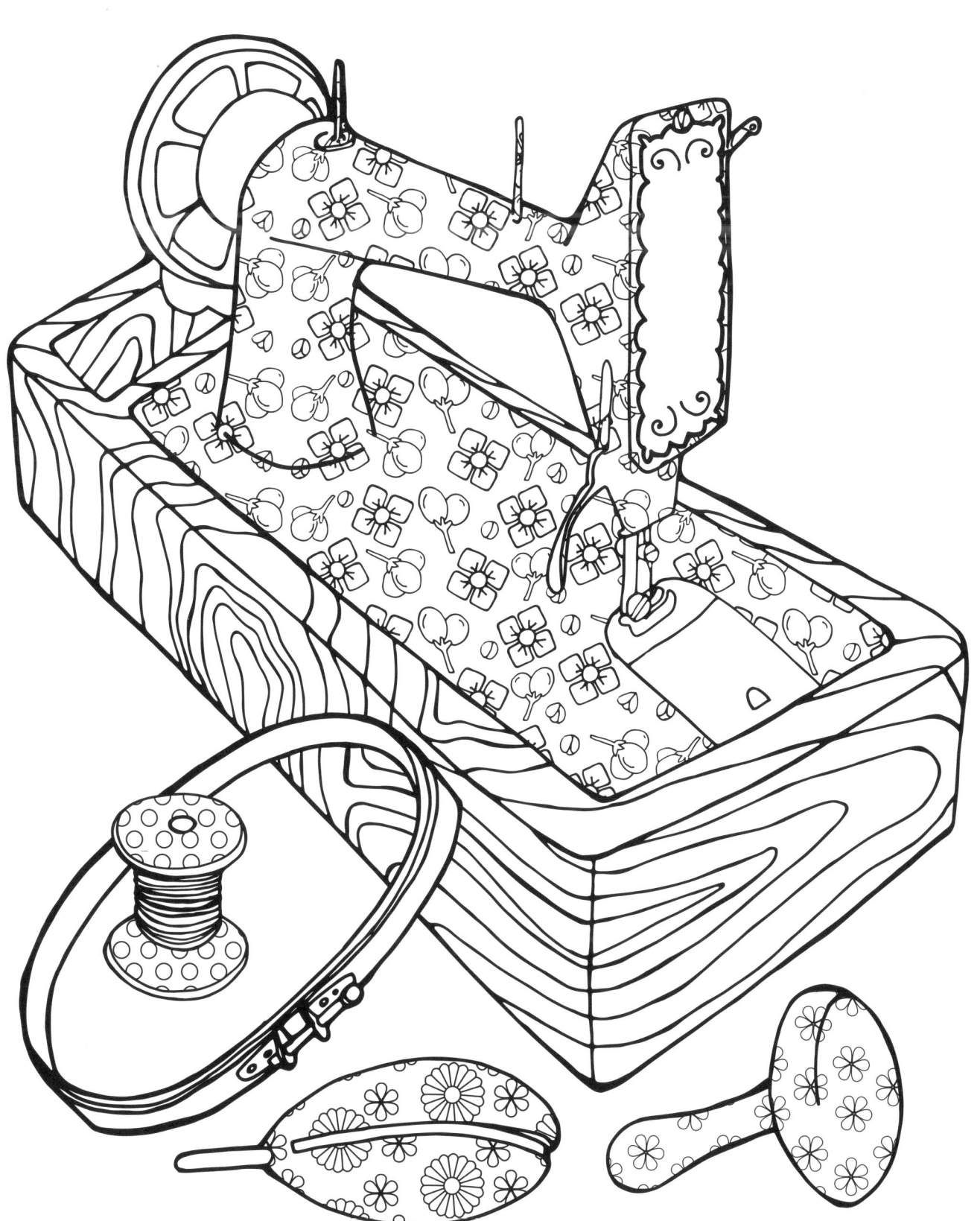

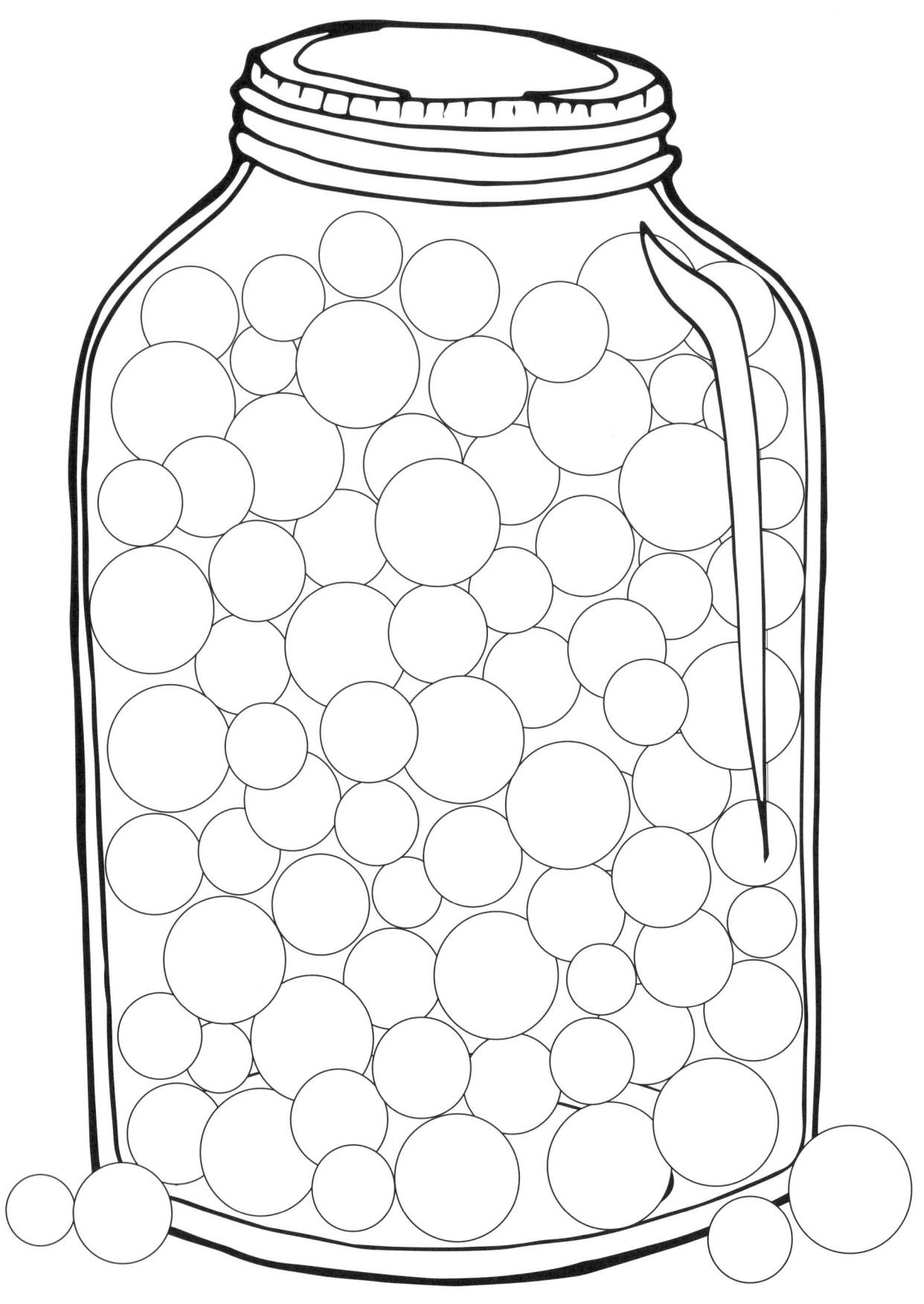

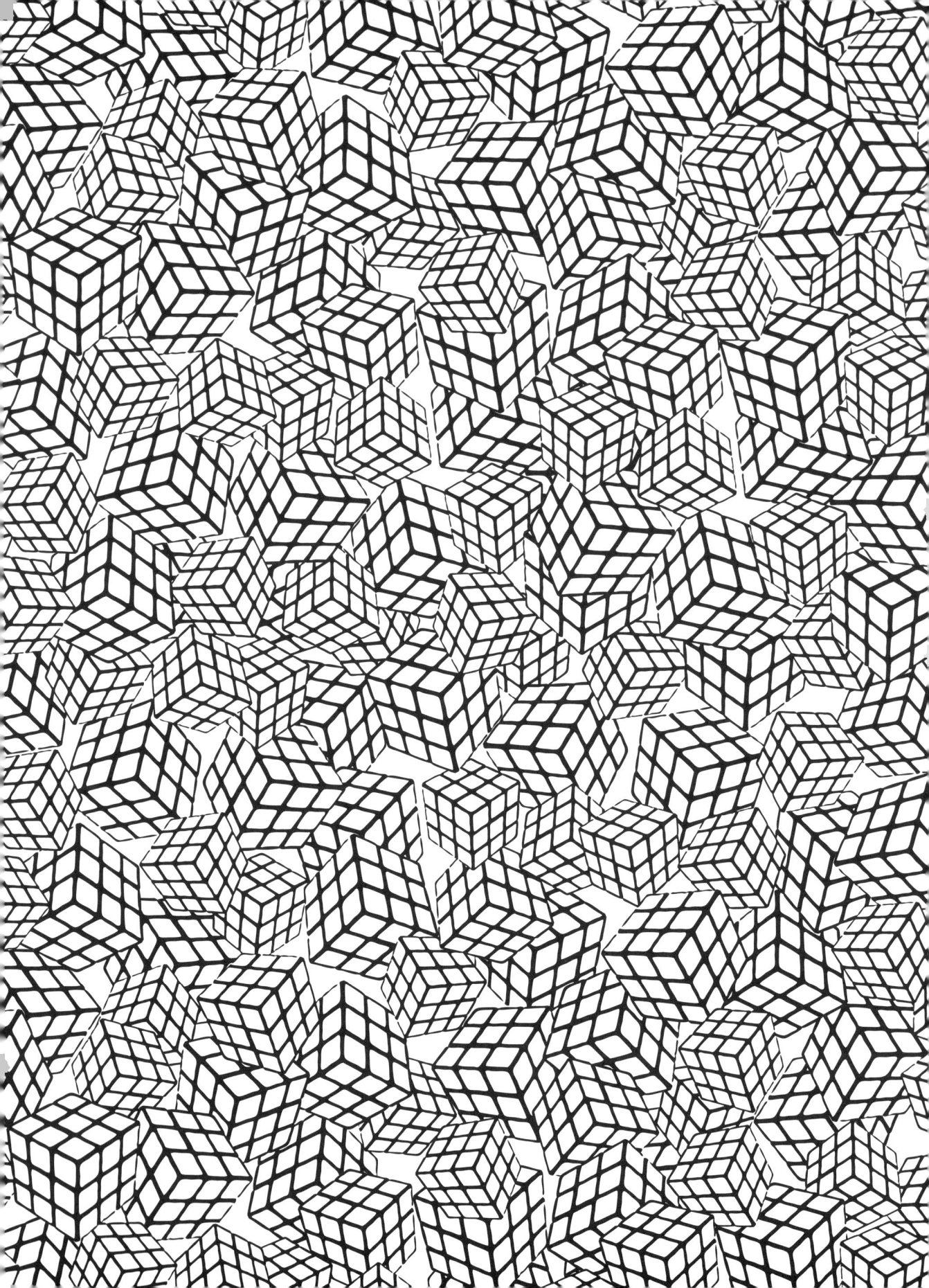

crazy flying sheep!

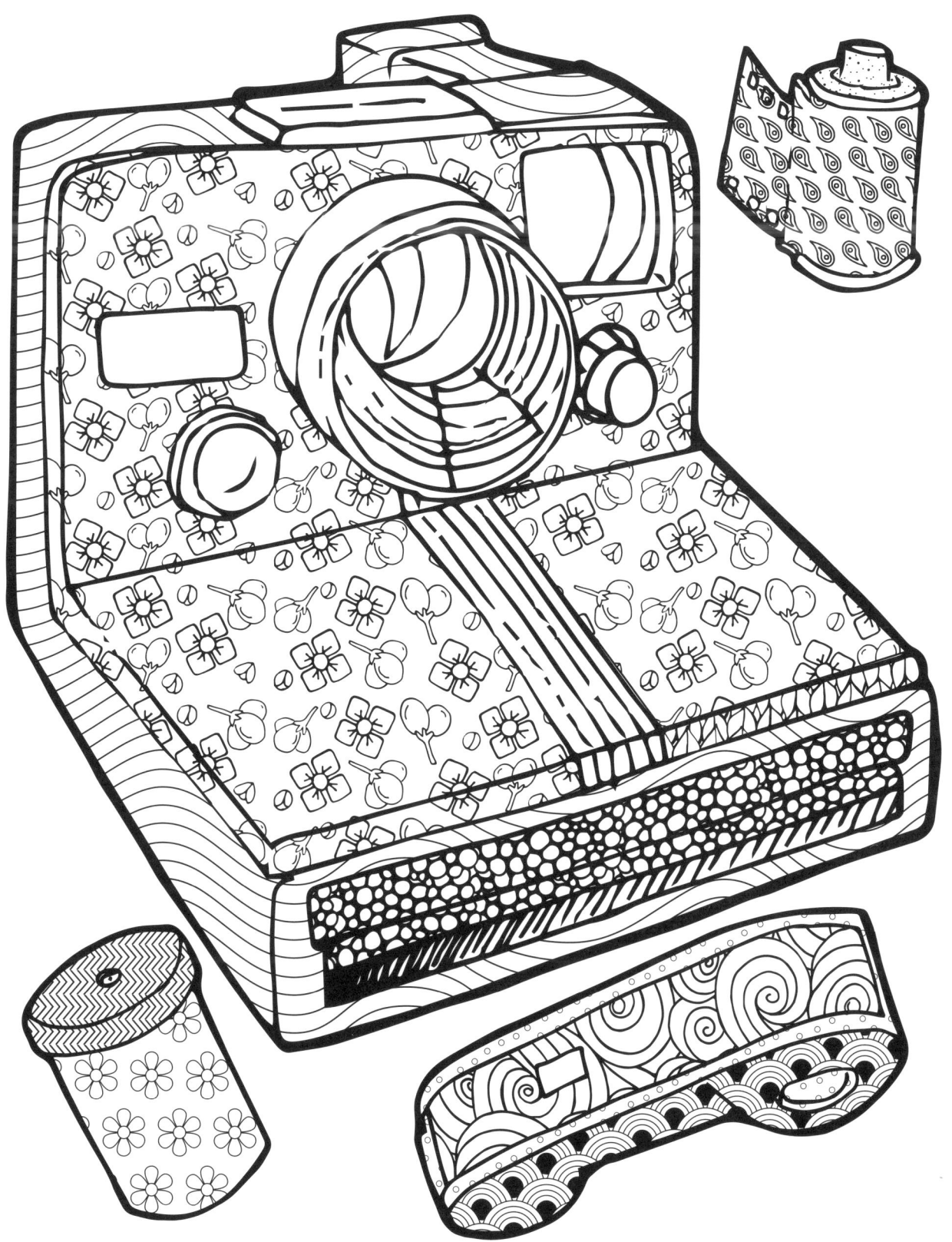

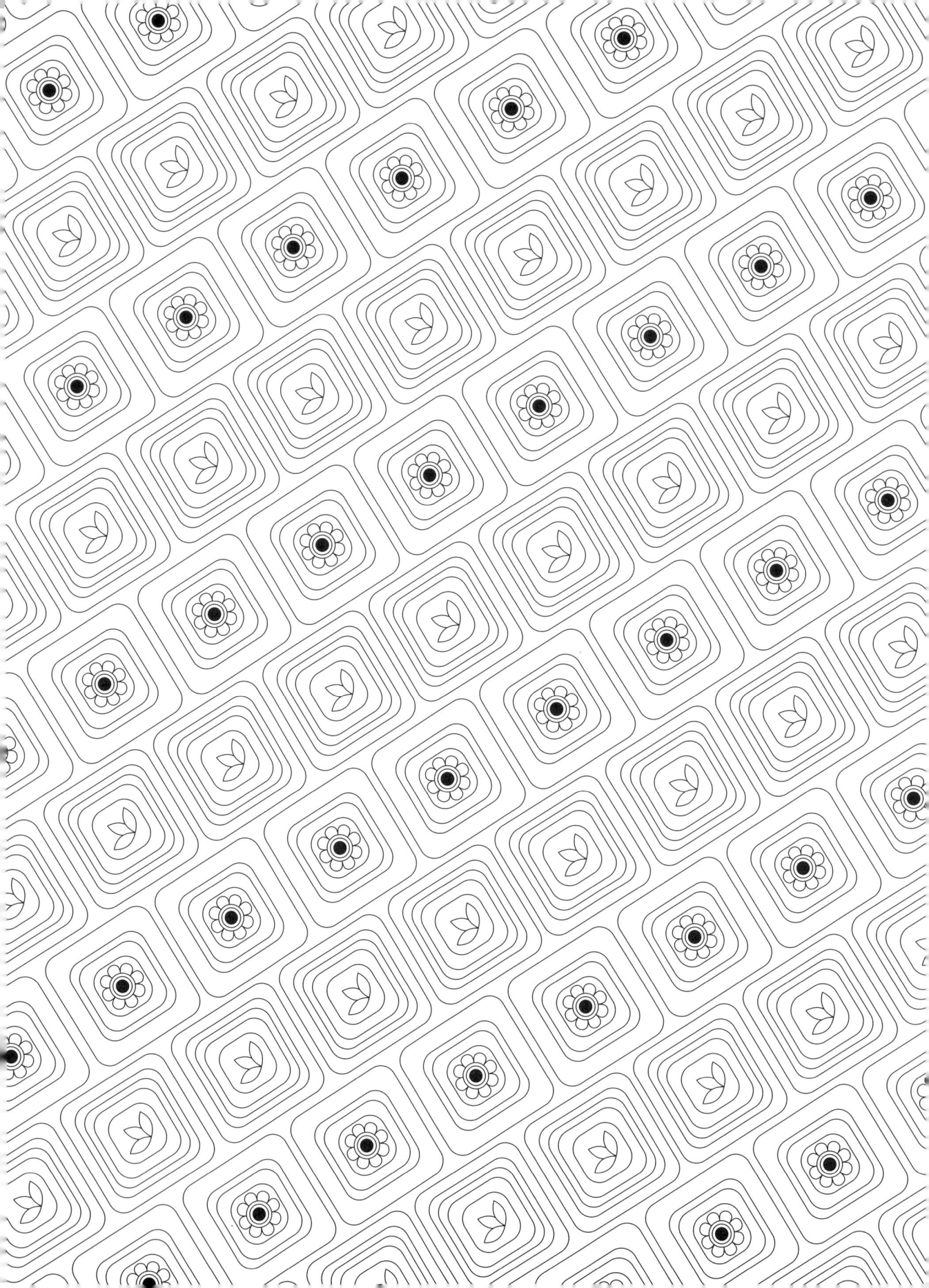

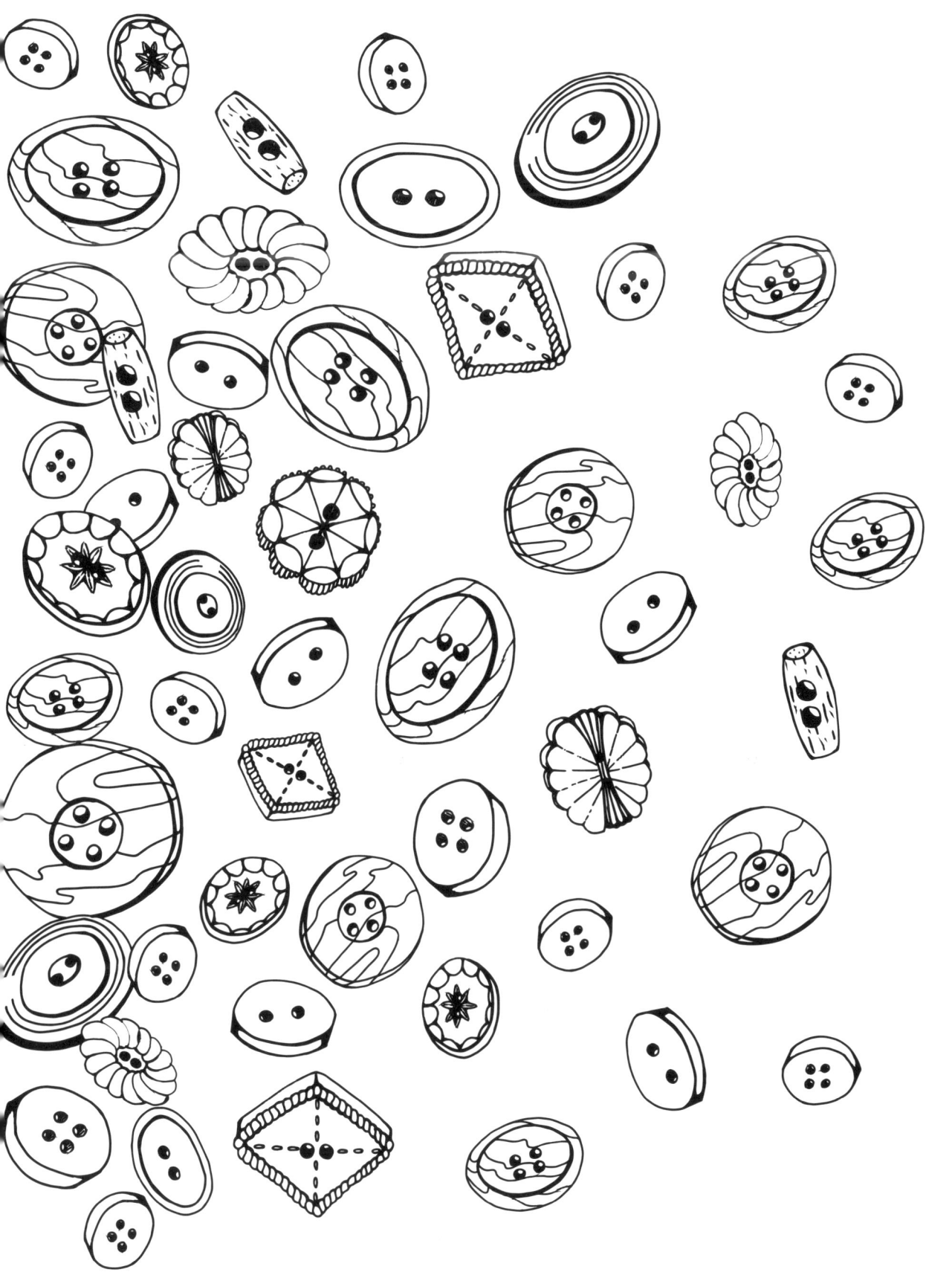

Do you remeber these?

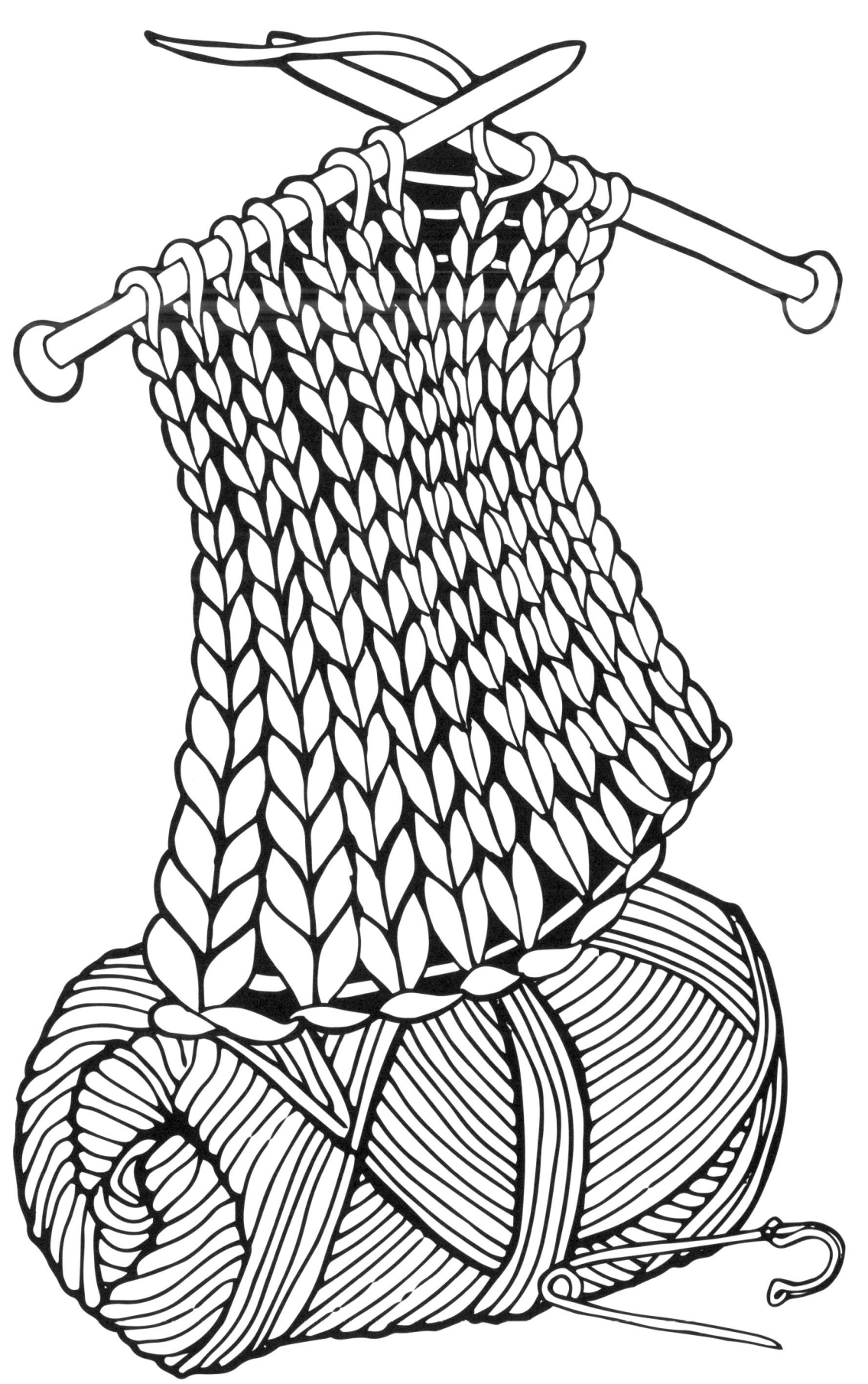

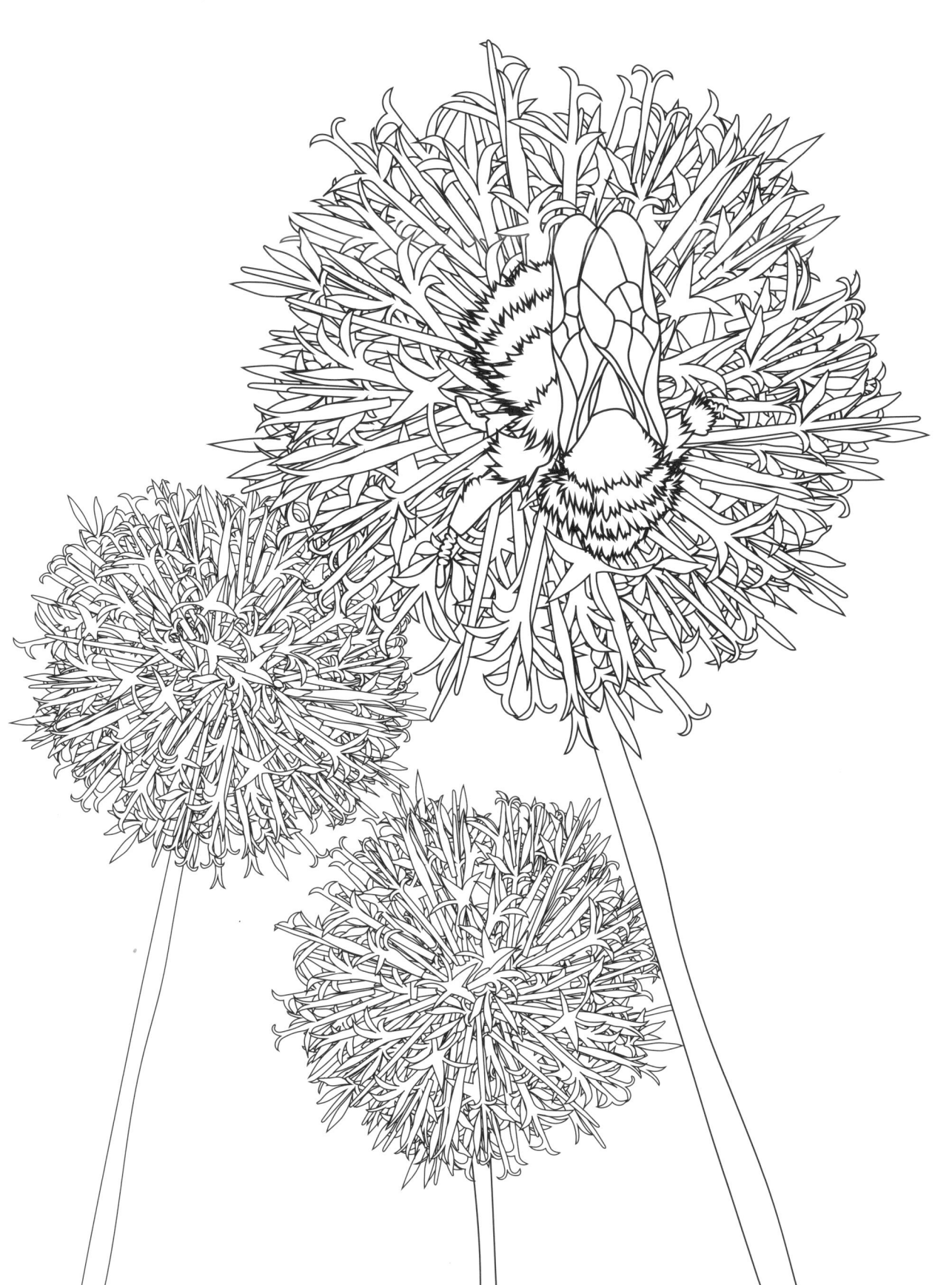

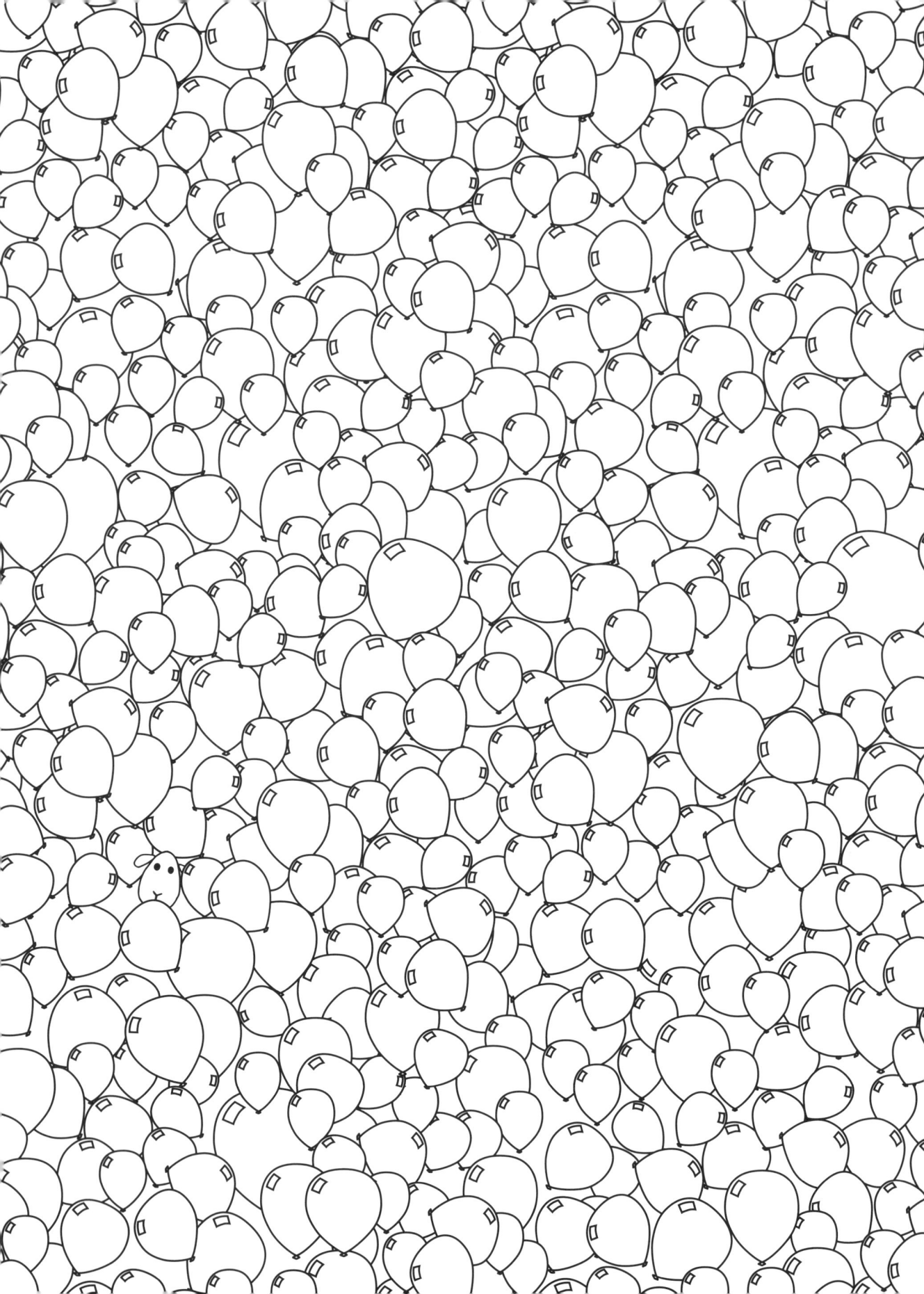

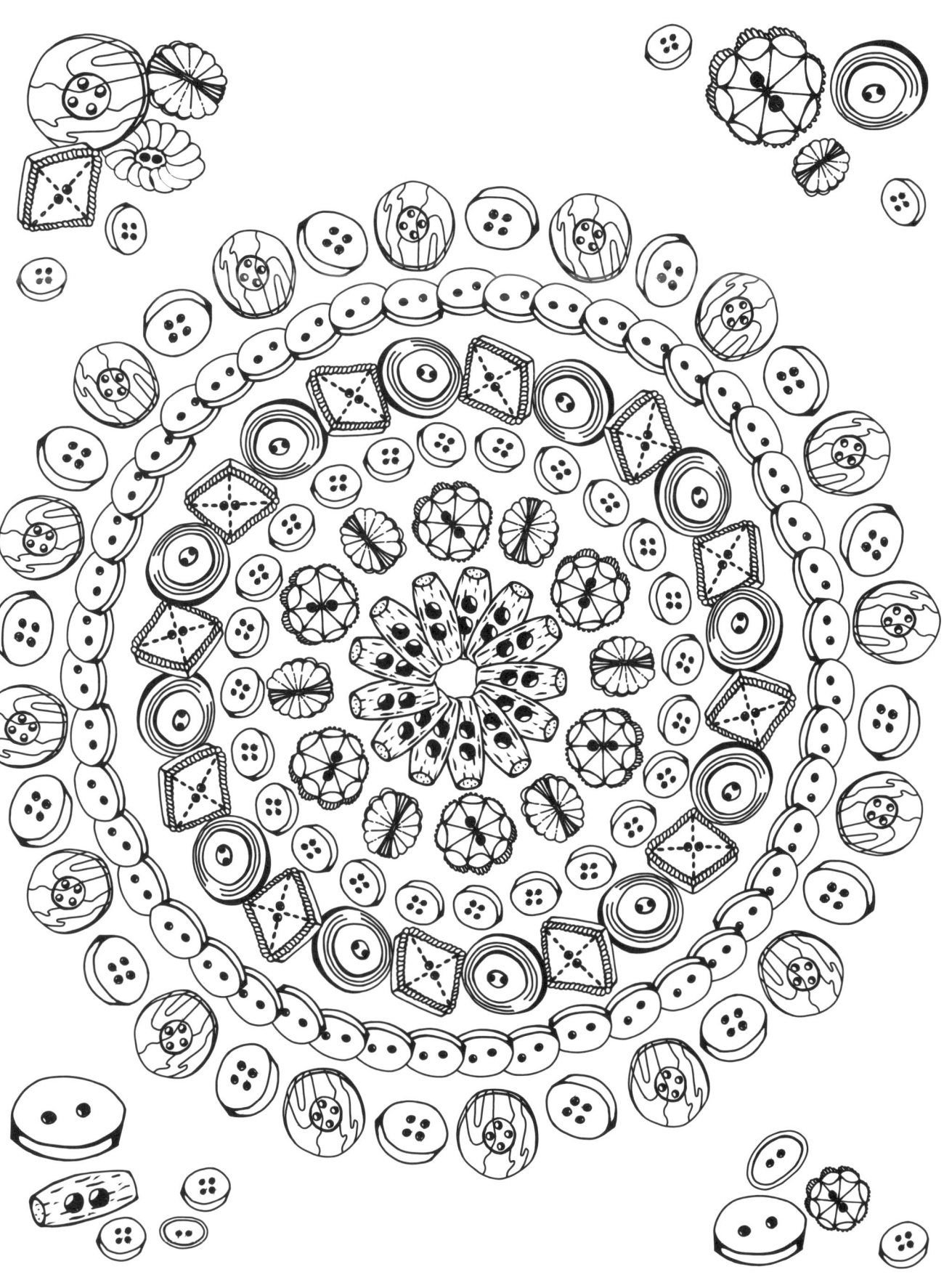

Hope you enjoyed the book, there's more to come!

Help me to help you by sending me feedback, and help me to help others by checking out the charity sites below

Charities close to my heart

www.aaa.uk.com - Raising awareness for Motor Neurone Disease

www.helpingrhinos.org - while they are still around

www.mpssociety.org.uk - For Sally & Ella

www.mndassociation.org - For Alie, Colin, Jensen & Phoenix

www.multiplesclerosis.net - For Dan

www.naomihouse.org.uk - for Ella

my Arty & Crafty friends.

www.richardsymonds.co uk - Wildlife artist & photographer.

www.thecraftingplace.co.uk - Fellow crafter in crime, all that is woolly.

www.raspberryrings.etsy.com - Glass jewellery designer.

Please post up photo's of your finished pages I would love to see them.

facebook: **crafty colouring**
instagram: **craftycolouring**